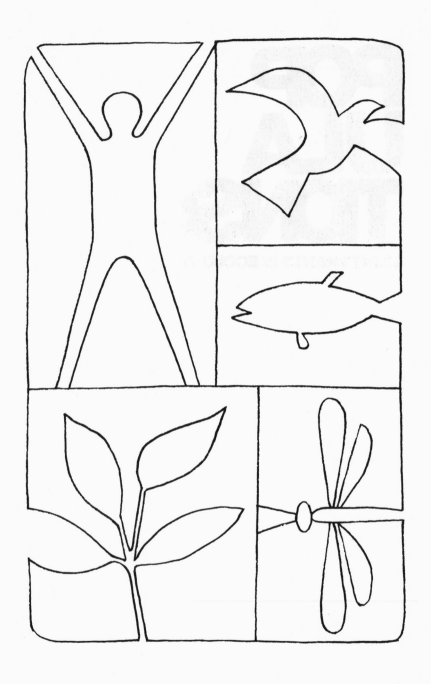

POP ULA TIONS:

EXPERIMENTS IN ECOLOGY

by A. Harris Stone
and Stephen Collins

illustrated by Peter P. Plasencia

Franklin Watts, Inc. New York · 1973

To Melody, Alex and Ben

*Illustration on page 50 rendered from a
photograph courtesy of United Press
International*

Library of Congress Cataloging in Publication Data

Stone, A.   Harris.
   Populations: experiments in ecology.

   SUMMARY: Simple problems and experiments demonstrate the
causes of population growth and decline among plants, animals, and
humans, means of predicting population trends, and effects of overpopulation on the environment.
      1.   Animal populations—Juvenile literature.
   2.   Ecology—Juvenile literature.   [1.   Population.
   2.   Ecology]   I.   Collins, Stephen, joint author.
   II.   Plasencia, Peter P., illus.   III   Title.
   QL752.S76   574.5'24   72-2303
   ISBN 0-531-02579-9

CONTENTS

POP ULA TIONS:

EXPERIMENTS IN ECOLOGY

INTRODUCTION

The Puzzling Picture of Population

How many angels can sit on the head of a pin? How many people are there on a train in which "people are packed in like sardines"? Are there more people in the city of New York than in the state of California? Which is more crowded: one square foot of ground in New York City or one square foot of ground in the Arizona desert on which two people are standing? These are questions that ask, "How many things or people can fit in a given place?"

There are other questions we could ask about what happens to people when there are too few or too many in a given place. For example, have you ever been on a very crowded elevator? How did you feel? Have you been all alone in the woods for three or four hours? How did you feel? The behavior of animals and plants is affected both by how many individuals there are and how much space is available to them. Imagine what might happen if fifty mice were placed in a shoebox. Would they be quiet and happy under such crowded conditions? Would they share food which was placed in the center of the box? How

1

would people act in equally crowded conditions? Would there be fights? Noise? Confusion? Would they share food?

This book is about how large or small numbers of plants and animals live together in a given space. Here you will find some ideas about the numbers of living things. This study of numbers of plants and animals may be called *population biology*. Most of the population ideas are approached in this book through doing some kind of experiment. Doing the experiments will help you understand the ideas that are presented. Perhaps, with some hard work and a little luck, you may find some ideas of your own.

INDIVIDUALS NEAR AND FAR

What is a Population?

A box of thumbtacks is a population. All of the carrots on a carrot farm are a population. All of the apple trees in an orchard are a population. All of the ring-tailed lemurs in Madagascar are a population. All of the Indians in America are a population. All of the red-haired, blue-eyed, 5-foot-11-inch-tall people of Polish extraction who live in St. Louis, Missouri, are a population. All of the corn flakes in a box are a population.

Each of these objects, plants, or animals is a population for a very specific reason. The word "population" has both its own definite meaning and unique meanings that come from the different ways in which people use the word. But, there are several specific characteristics which define the word "population." The first characteristic of the word "population" is as follows: All of the ————in a specific or given————. Here the first blank refers to a description of a group or set of objects, plants, or animals; for example, all of the people, spiders, bluebirds, rifles, or trains. The second blank describes the space, or area, in which they exist; for example, all of

3

the given————in a specific continent, country, state, field, barn, box, or jar.

Another characteristic of populations is the number of objects that the population describes. Four carrots may be a population. Four million carrots may also be a population. Just as the number of objects is part of the definition of a population, so is the area or space in which the objects are found. For example, "four carrots in a box" is one idea of population. "Four carrots in the world" is a different idea of population.

Finally, the object, the number of objects, the space, and the amount of space, all have names. These names are an important part of the definition of a population. For example, we could say all the plants on Farmer Jones's farm, which would include many different plants, are the plant population. This would refer not only to the carrot population of the farm but also to the corn population and the beet population and all of the other crops that Farmer Jones grows.

The use of the word "population" must be both broad and encompassing and at the same time strict and narrow, if it is to be understood in all of the many ways in which it is usually used. An example of these definitions of population may help you understand both the broad and narrow use of the word. Here are nine distinct populations:

1. All the oranges in the world.
2. All the oranges in the United States.
3. All the oranges in California.
4. All the oranges in Robin County.
5. All the oranges on the Martin farm.
6. All the oranges in a bushel basket.
7. All the oranges on the table.
8. All the oranges in your stomach.
9. All the oranges in your hand.

Now let's look more closely at some major ideas about populations.

HOW MANY, HOW CLOSE?

Population Density

How many marbles can you put in a medicine vial? Is the vial full after you put as many marbles as you can into it? Can you add any water to a vial that is "full" of marbles? If you can add water to a vial full of marbles, was the vial full? If the marbles had been water, how many more marbles could have been placed in the vial?

How many pieces of chalk can you place in a vial? Try it. Smash up the chalk into a powder and try again. How many pieces of powdered chalk can fit in the same vial? How much water can you put into a balloon? What happens to the balloon as you place more and more water into it?

A TIGHT SQUEEZE

Overpopulation

In a natural population, the numbers remain stable. As the older members of the population die, new members are born. All ages of animals or plants are represented in a stable population. The resources upon which a stable population depends are never depleted, but are constantly replenished. This is the situation which people have in mind when they speak of the "balance of nature."

When the balance of nature is destroyed, the population can become too small or it can become too large.

Low population density is a rare occurrence in nature. If man has greatly lowered the number of animals in a given area by killing them or destroying their food supply, it is possible that the remaining members of the population will be so widely scattered that they would be unable to locate each other during mating season and thus produce no offspring. Animals, however, have many unique ways of sensing each other's presence by their keen senses of smell, vision, and hearing. Unless they are greatly influenced by man, we can assume that natural populations are seldom affected by low population density.

A far more common consequence of the disturbing of the balance of nature is overpopulation. Overpopulation can occur when a species is living in an undisturbed state, but it is usually a temporary condition and nature brings things back into balance. In most populations, a harmful increase in numbers is due to man having changed something in the environment of the plants or animals. For example, if a population of natural predators is hunted down, their prey will suffer from overpopulation.

Overpopulation has many effects. In areas where the natural predators of deer, such as mountain lions, have been severely reduced, the deer population has become crowded. The deer soon deplete the most nourishing plants by eating them faster than plant growth restores them and the population becomes underweight. The deer turn to "stuffing" foods of limited nutritional value. They may even browse on poisonous plants. The female deer often have only a single fawn instead of twins or triplets. The male deer usually grow smaller-sized antlers.

The most obvious sign of an area overpopulated by deer or their relatives is a "browse line." This is the height above which the deer cannot reach twigs and buds. Below the browse line, all the valuable living plant food has been eaten. The browse line moves to greater heights as the deer continue to consume all the food that they can reach by standing on their hind legs.

Inside the deer, the adrenal glands, which grow very large in populations that are crowded, may enlarge three to five times. Following the overcrowded conditions, the deer population crashes into a decline. Too many deer cause suffering for all members of the population. Hardest hit are the smaller animals, particularly fawns, which cannot reach the food above the browse line. It takes many years of relief from the "overbrowsing" for woody plants to recover their normal growth. It also takes many years for a population of deer to come back to normal.

A CIRCULAR TRACK

Population Turnover

Get a pencil and paper and imagine these situations: You have two pet gerbils in a cage that measures two square feet. They are male and female. One day you find out that the gerbils had eight babies. Calculate the population density the day before they had babies and the day after they had babies, and count each baby as an individual. What has happened to the population density because of the newborn gerbils? Imagine that the newborn gerbils grow up and become the mature offspring of these parents, and that your friends take a liking to your gerbils. Suppose you give each of your friends a pair of your gerbils. What has happened to the population density when you give away the first pair of gerbils? The second pair of gerbils? The third pair of gerbils? The fourth pair of gerbils? Graph the population density so that each time you give away one pair of gerbils, you show the new population density. Assume that you kept all the gerbils in the same cage in which they were born.

After you have given away all of the children of the original pair of gerbils and you have only the original pair left, you can imagine that the parent gerbils will eventually become old and die. What happens to the population density when one of the parents dies? When both of the parents die? How can the population density be increased after both parent gerbils die?

Let us look at another case of population turnover. Suppose we have the original parents and their eight offspring, and before any offspring are given away, the parents die. Is the population density different when the parents die than when you give away two of the offspring before the parents die? The number of individuals in a population in a given space determines the population density. But *which* individuals are present is a factor that is described in population turnover. It does not matter whether you have parents and six offspring, for a total of eight individuals in a cage, or just eight offspring—the population density is the same. However, in the second case the population has turned over because two of the original gerbils have gone and two different ones have taken their place.

What evidence is there that population turnover takes place in your town? Has there been any population turnover in your home during the past ten or fifteen years? What changes have taken place in your town which are a result of population turnover? What changes have taken place in your school class?

A population may consist of mostly the same individuals, or constantly undergo change as old individuals die and new ones take their places. A population which is turning over quickly usually has more youthful members than older members. A farmer who raises frying chickens needs to be able to produce a bird which is young and tender rather than old and tough. He will manage his

flock of chickens in such a way that no bird is allowed to become too old and thus will always have a high population turnover.

In nature, vigorous strong animals get along better than crippled, diseased, old, weak, or young animals. There is a limit to the number of animals which an area can support. The death of one animal provides more food for the remaining animals. With high population turnover, there is a youthful population which produces more offspring. Then there is more new growth, and if conditions in the environment change to allow for more individuals, the population can become larger very quickly.

Adaptation to a changing environment happens most quickly when the population experiences a high number of replacements. Flies for example produce many generations in a short period of time. When DDT was first sprayed where houseflies lived, their populations soon developed immunity to the original doses of the insecticide. The stronger flies that survived the insecticide had offspring that were better adapted to living in the presence of DDT and soon the entire population was resistant to the chemical.

Population turnover is usually higher for small organisms with many generations produced in a short time, than for large organisms which take a long time to reach breeding age and need to reach a large size before they mature.

SIR OR MADAM?

Sex Ratios

What percentage of a very large population is female? The most direct way to find out, without counting every single individual, is to count some of the members of the population. The group that is counted is called a sample. By separating according to sex, and counting all members of the sample, you can calculate the male-female sex ratios of a population. This can be a difficult task with some plants and animals, so find the ratio by counting male and female people.

Does the location at which you count have an effect on the ratio that you find? Try making several counts at such different locations as a supermarket, an office building, a building construction site, and a movie. Does the time of day at which the count is made have any effect on the ratio that is found? What effect on the ratio is found if the count is made for a short period of time? A long period of time? A chart such as the one shown here will help you compare places, times, and sex ratios.

		Male	Female	Female %	Male %
Place	Time				
	Time				
	Time				
Place	Time				
	Time				
	Time				

What is the sex ratio of chickens on this page?

In many populations the ratio between males and females determines the ratio at which the population can grow. Which group of chickens shown here would reproduce most rapidly?

The male-female ratio is a number which compares the number of males to the number of females. At the time of birth, the sex ratio is usually about fifty-fifty, which means that there is one male born for every one female born. Actually, in many species, there are more males produced than females, but the infant death rate among males may be higher.

Because one male can simultaneously father many offspring, nature seems determined to save females rather than males. We see this in the duller colors of female birds. Their color makes it difficult to see them and so they are better protected from predators than the males. Females also have sharper hunting instincts. The female domestic cat is an excellent hunter, and if she were living in nature, she would be the sole provider of food for her young kittens.

Both males and females are needed for reproduction, and the ability to produce offspring is essential to survival of a population. Therefore, it is more important to have a surplus of females than a surplus of males. For hunters there is a law called the buck law which allows hunters to kill only male deer and only those with antlers of a certain size. The doe deer then outnumber the bucks, and both the food and space required by a buck can be used instead by fawns and does.

Among seals, a bachelor herd often remains off by itself while a few bulls dominate and serve as fathers for many females. The bachelor seals must fight the old bulls for the right to become fathers, and only the strongest, most aggressive males can win. This assures that the race of seals will be vigorous and strong if the quality called strength is inherited.

Among animals it is possible to see the difference between sexes because one sex is larger than the other, or it bears antlers, or it has brighter feathers. Sometimes, the difference is only in a single marking. If a male moustache mark is artificially made on a female bird called a flicker, she will be attacked by a male who no longer recognizes her as a female bird. Among mammals, the males are usually heavier and larger. Among birds, males usually wear the bright colors and the females are often smaller. However, birds of prey, such as hawks and owls, depend upon strength for capturing food, and the female may be as much as one-third larger than the male.

HOW YOUNG, HOW MANY?

Age Profiles

Are there more high-school girls or more grandfathers in your town? How many men in your town are between the ages of twenty and thirty? How many women are between forty and fifty? If all of the people in a population are separated into age groups, a chart showing the "groups of ages" can be made. This chart is called an age profile.

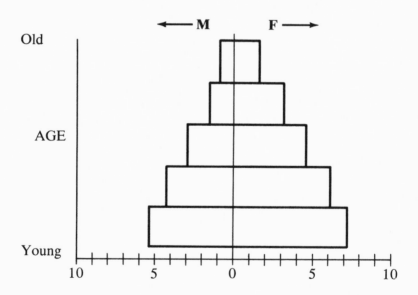

Make an age profile of the people in your town. The information for making such a chart can be found at your city hall in the census data. Is this information up to date? Can you obtain the same information for an age profile by counting and classifying people at a downtown intersection? What differences are there between the estimated age profile and the one made from census information?

An age profile is a diagram that shows the groups of individuals in given age categories. It looks like a pyramid because few individuals in a population live to a very old age, so there are fewer of them. This is shown at the top of the pyramid. When an age profile looks like a pyramid with a broad base, it is because there are more young people in the population, and the younger the age class the more members it has. This means that there are always less five-year-olds than two-year-olds, and always less thirty-year-olds than twenty-year-olds. If an age profile becomes narrow at any point, it means that that age class has fewer members. In the United States, for instance, people had smaller families in the 1930s, and so an age profile has a narrow place at one age group. It looks as if someone put a belt on it and pulled it tight.

In countries where people do not know how to limit the size of their families, or for some reason will not limit the size of their families, age profiles look like a pyramid with a very broad base. In such a country the children are the largest part of the population. If a profile looks like an evergreen tree, the constricted base of the pyramid means that the people have recently decided to limit their population.

Many ideas about how people live can be learned just by looking at an age profile. For example, in countries where there are large percentages of very young and very old people, there is probably a smaller group called workers who must support the old and the young. The profile tells how many workers there are and how many people are too young or too old to work. If there are too many young and too many old people, it may mean that very young children will *have* to work. Another example

of what can be learned from a profile is the information about the rate at which a population will grow. If a population has mostly young adults of childbearing age, then the population is likely to grow much more rapidly than it would if there were more mature adults and older persons.

The age profile is a picture-graph that tells something about a population's makeup in terms of ages and sex. When we know the details of a population structure, we can draw conclusions about past events such as wars or famines which may have changed the profile. We may also be able to predict what will happen to growth patterns in the future.

SIX-HUNDRED SIXTY OR ONE?

The Limitations of Resources

How many plants and animals can live in a given area? What effect does the size of these organisms have on how many can survive? These questions can be answered by finding out whether a given number of large plants grow as well in a pot of soil as the same number of small plants. Will a pound of soil support the growth of fifty lima-bean plants as well as a pound of the same soil supports the growth of fifty grass plants? How much smaller is one grass plant than one lima-bean plant?

What effect is seen if equal-size pots are used? If different-size pots are used?

Space is limited, but living things can produce endless numbers of offspring; that is, until they run out of something essential such as air, food, or space. The exact time when that will happen is never known because the effects of not enough food or air or space develop gradually. What can be seen is that each generation appears a little less vigorous. Each new generation appears stunted or below average in some way. The effect could be that a new generation has increased susceptibility to some disease.

The choice that organisms have is quite simple—there can be a few large organisms or many small ones. A good example is a fishpond. Suppose that the pond can support two hundred pounds of fish. The weight of the fish that can stay alive in the pond can be called the weight limit. There could be ten thousand minnow-sized fish in the pond if their total weight was two hundred pounds. Or there could be one hundred two-pound fish. People are interested in fish for food and so they prefer to have bigger fish in a pond. Anyone who has ever cleaned a fish knows that it is a lot easier to clean a big fish than a little fish. And certainly a big fish has more fight on the end of a fishing pole than a small one. So it is important to have some way of cutting down the numbers of small fish, and provide the conditions which will allow the remaining fish to grow to a size we call harvestable.

Here is another example of size and space. Our Western prairies supported millions of bison before the white hunters eliminated most of them. If a bison weighs

two thousand pounds and a prairie dog weighs three
pounds, and if we had a choice of which animals were to
inhabit an area, we could choose between 660 prairie
dogs or one bison. Here we assume that both mammals
feed on equal kinds of food. A prairie dog weighs thirty
times more than a meadow mouse. Again, if we assume
that both these mammals eat the same kind of food, then
each prairie dog would consume the food normally eaten
by thirty meadow mice. Another animal that eats the
same food is the grasshopper. If a grasshopper weighs

one-hundredth as much as a meadow mouse, then one hundred grasshoppers eat the equivalent of one mouse. With these numbers, you can figure out how many grasshoppers it would take to eat the equivalent of one bison's food for a day.

MAJORITY RULE?

Competition and Population

What happens when two different organisms in an environment have very similar needs? Can two species live compatibly if both have the same growth needs? Try growing lettuce seeds in a pot of soil that has been taken directly from a plot of grass. Use two pots so that one can be weeded and one not weeded. Does the lettuce grow well when weeds are constantly picked out and thrown away? What happens to the lettuce if no weeds are pulled out?

Before white settlers arrived in North America, the native Indians were the only humans living there. They wasted little. Their trash heaps must have been small. The Indian shared his environment with native mice and with the gentle wood rat, another native mammal. When the white man arrived, his ships carried rats and mice that traveled with him from European ports. One kind of rat that he brought was the black rat, whose fleas carry the deadly bubonic plague. This disease killed millions of people and had once shrunk the population of Europe to a third of its former numbers. The black rat could not swim to North America, but once it arrived here its population grew, particularly in the ports of the Eastern seaboard. The black rat could only live successfully by using buildings and homes for shelter and by eating stored grains. The Indian could supply neither of these requirements for the black rat. In other words, the white settler created an environment, or an ecological niche, for his unwanted companion, the black rat.

Biologists have long recognized that it is almost impossible for two different species of organisms to occupy the same niche. One of them is usually more fit than the other, and the more fit one will survive, prosper, compete with, and finally displace the less fit organism. Just as the black rat was settling into its niche, ships began to arrive in this country with the brown, or Norway, rat which is more aggressive than the black rat. This spelled the end for the large populations of black rats. The brown rats took their place. Today, the brown rat has spread into almost all parts of North America. The black rat is a rarity except in a few seaports where it is found now and then. Brown rats dominate everywhere.

The rule that two organisms cannot continue to occupy the same niche is proved by the story of the black and the brown rat in North America. If the black rat had the flexibility to live in niches away from human shelter and food supply, perhaps it could have become a naturalized citizen of North America along with the brown rat and its lesser cousin, the house mouse.

MORE THAN ENOUGH

Survival of a Species

Did the earth always have 3,600,000,000 people? If not, how did so many people come from so few? How many fruit flies are there in the world? How long does it take for ten fruit flies in a jar to produce a "jarful" of fruit flies?

You can catch the first ten fruit flies by using the fly trap shown here. Clear plastic sheets can be used to make the funnel. A dish of mashed bananas provides good bait for attracting the flies. Place the trap on a windowsill for several days.

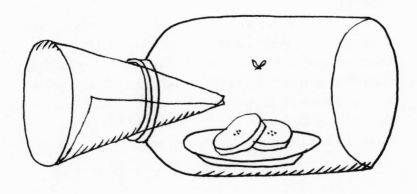

To breed more flies from the first ten, a large jar with mashed bananas can be used. How many flies are there after ten days? Twenty days? Thirty days?

In nature, one individual is not as important as a population because individuals are born and die, but the population continues. Also, among the higher animals, an individual cannot reproduce by itself. What *is* important is the population, whether it is large or small. The population may change in size, but as long as there remain enough individuals within it who can reproduce their kind, the population has the ingredients for success.

Built into the workings of every species is the virtual command always to produce more offspring than can possibly ever survive in the given surroundings. Man is like other animals in being able to produce far more offspring than can survive. Most creatures that produce surplus offspring lack the power to change and control their environments to accommodate the surplus young. Man alone has the skills and culture to change his environment to allow his children to survive. In this way he has temporarily destroyed the limitations on his own numbers.

Let us consider what happens to two families of humans after five generations have been born. One family, which we will call the Smiths, produces only two children each time a member marries. The other family, named Green, produces twelve children each time a member marries. Let us assume that at the end of five generations all of the last three generations are alive.

Generations of the Smiths		1	2	3	4	5
# of individuals	2	4	8	16	32	64
Parents					112 living	

If the last three generations of the Smiths are living, we now have 112 people.

Now let us consider the Greens:

Generations of the Greens

	1	2	3	4	5
2	12	144	1,728	20,736	248,832
Parents				271,296 living	

There are more than a quarter of a million Greens in the last three generations, but only 112 of the Smiths. The Greens have increased at a much faster "rate" than the Smiths. Their rapid increase in numbers is called a geometric progression.

The Smiths are outnumbered by the Greens by a factor of about three thousand. If all Greens continue to have twelve children in each generation and each of these children has twelve children, the total number of Greens in the family becomes staggering. From this example we see that humans who have more than two children increase the size of the population at a very rapid rate. Some scientists have determined that if each family has only two children, the total size of the population will not increase or decrease. Are the scientists correct?

MANY TOO MANY

Natural Population Controls

Will fruit flies in a jar reproduce continually until the jar is packed solid with fruit flies? If they could, would the packing effect kill all of the flies? Try finding out if a vast number of fruit flies can exist in a jar without destroying themselves. Take ten fruit flies and let them breed in a jar. Use a piece of mashed banana for food and wait

about a month. Divide all of the flies into ten new breeding jars. Wait another month and place the flies from all ten jars into one new breeding jar with food. Does breeding continue after this point? How long does breeding continue?

Nature seems to arrange that more offspring will be produced than can possibly survive. It's almost as if life is a giant contest—many can enter the game, but the numbers of winners are limited. This is not wasteful when one realizes that many of the losers become food for other organisms. Although an oak tree might produce thousands of acorns each year and millions before it dies, there is room in the forest for only a few mighty oaks. Countless generations of squirrels, mice, and acorn weevils are nourished by all those acorns that failed to grow into oak trees. So the process of "too many" in nature is part of a total food web that links many kinds of living things together.

Sometimes, however, nature learns to economize. Consider two kinds of voles—one the meadow vole, the other the yellow-nosed vole. Each vole is a stubby kind of mouse that feeds mostly on plant food. Each occupies a different habitat. The meadow vole lives in grassy meadows where its runways lace the grass and its domed grassy nests are vulnerable to any animal powerful enough to part the grass. The meadow vole can have as many as ten young each time it reproduces. And it can produce as many as seventeen litters every year. Females may begin to breed when they are three weeks old. The yellow-nosed vole is a woodland species which nests in dens protected by a pile of stones. A skunk or a fox cannot dig up such nests because of the rocks. The yellow-nosed voles have litters of only three or four young. In the case of each of these species of mice, we see an evolutionary adjustment to the chance of destruction. With their better protection, the yellow-nosed vole can survive by producing fewer offspring.

Nature's rules against having too many organisms surviving are strict. One way that we can study the rules is to create some questions to think about.

How many is too many?
At what point are there "too many"?
Why are there too many?

If you think about these questions they may lead you to others. What happens when organisms run out of something? What is that important something? Is it food? Is it space? Is it peace and quiet? Is it the same thing for all organisms? Can an organism run out of only *one* thing and be limited from further reproduction or must it run out of several things before its numbers become limited?

TOGETHER WE STAND

Aggregation

Mr. Greenthumb has four fields which border each other. Where the four corners meet there stands a large acorn-producing oak tree. Each of the fields around the tree has oak seedlings growing in different patterns. The seedlings in one field were distributed mainly by gray squirrels who buried the acorns as a way of storing food. The seedlings in the second field came mainly from acorns that fell or were blown from the tree. In the third field the acorns fell into old plow furrows. In the fourth field the acorns fell as they did in the second field; however, the fourth field had a steep slope away from the tree. Look at the dots which represent seedlings in each of the fields and decide which field has the slope, which had the squirrels, which had the furrows, and which had acorns that merely fell on the ground. Does the sloping field have either a gully or a ridge in it? Can you determine the direction of the prevailing winds?

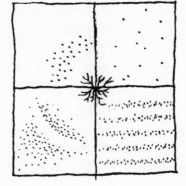

We are able to study how plants in four adjoining fields are distributed by various forces and conditions because the young seedlings do not move from their landing places. There are also distribution patterns among animals, but since most animals can choose their locations by moving, animal distribution can change from minute to minute according to factors which vary.

Animals may come together, or aggregate, for many reasons. A herd of musk oxen often form a circle on the arctic snow. With their heads lowered and facing outward, the adult musk oxen surround the calves inside a protective circle. This helps to protect the young against attacks by wolves.

Studies of wolves show that when they hunt large prey, such as moose, they gain a hunting advantage by aggregating in packs. Even as a pack, however, they cannot successfully kill such large prey unless it is weakened by hunger, disease, or injury. If a moose has a disease, and if the wolves eat that moose, the disease is kept from spreading to healthy moose.

When young rabbits huddle together in their nest, they share each other's warmth. In this way they conserve energy that might otherwise be spent. Energy not needed for keeping warm may help the young rabbits grow more rapidly, or demand less milk from the mother rabbit. The mother conserves her energy by being able to feed all of the young in one place—she does not have to travel in order to take care of her offspring.

Seabirds sometimes form floating lines in the water, and starlings often form lines walking over ground where they hunt their food. This systematic combing of an area yields more food by not wasting time hunting over ground which has already been searched. It may also function as a "drive" which flushes out prey.

If you watch dogs, pigeons, and other common animals, you may see examples of animals that stand together or feed together. Try to figure out why they are together.

A MEASURED GUESS

Predicting Populations

Measuring is useful in helping to understand a problem. In population studies, for example, we may want to know how many individuals there are in a given area, category, or population. Luckily, we do not have to count each individual if we will settle for knowing approximately how many there are. Sampling and predicting are techniques used to make approximations. Here is a problem where prediction is used to find the number of individuals in a population that cannot be directly counted at the time the number is determined:

Happy Days Elementary School has children in grades kindergarten through six. There are different numbers of children in each grade.

	Boys	Girls	Total
K	43	46	89
1	40	39	79
2	48	49	98
3	48	59	107
4	52	43	95
5	41	46	87
6	47	43	90

The question is, "How many children will there be in next year's kindergarten class?" To be sure, we cannot know exactly how many. But we can approximate the number by using the numbers in the chart. Will there be eighty-nine kindergarten children next year? Will the number next year be closer to the number now in kindergarten or the number now in grade three?

Predicting is guessing what will happen before it happens. Predicting the size of future populations of people is difficult because there are many different factors which affect the population. It is often a simple matter to predict how large a population of redwood trees, or deer, can develop because these wild species respond to natural forces which limit their population. Species such as redwoods and deer have stabilized their population. For example, deer populations have risen and fallen so often that scientists, by knowing about the food supply, the number of predators, and other factors, can accurately predict the upper limit of deer able to survive in a square mile.

There are many different ways to study the numbers of animals in order to make predictions. Consider the pheasant which often responds to a sudden explosion, such as a firecracker, by crowing. A count of the birds which crow at different locations immediately after a planned explosion can be done year after year from a series of fixed locations. If more birds crow at more locations in one year than another year, the assumption is that the population is larger. If few birds respond by crowing, the population is assumed to be lower. Sometimes a scientist merely wants to know whether a population is increasing or decreasing, and such a technique gives him a fairly good idea of whether the population is going up, down, or holding steady.

The population of humans is expanding everywhere in the world. Predicting the growth curve of people may give some clues about future human populations. When such estimates have been made in the past, they have usually been in error by estimating too few people. What factors have, or could, upset predictions on the growth of the human population?

WHAT IT TAKES

Consuming Resources

Counting the number of individuals in a population is only one kind of counting in population studies. We can also count the weight of biological materials in the food chain that supports each individual. How many ounces of food does a dog eat in one day? Suppose a dog eats one pound of food each day. Where did that food come from? One pound of beef is made by a cow eating eight pounds of grass. This means that the dog ate the equivalent of approximately eight pounds of grass.

Calculate the total weight of biological material that was used to produce your dinner.

Ratio: Food to Grass Item	Food Item	Weight		Equivalent in Grass
1:8	Beef	½ lb.	=	4 lbs. of grass
1:1	Potatoes	¼ lb.	=	?
1:1	Beans	¼ lb.	=	?
1:8	Milk	1 lb.	=	?
1:1	Apple	¼ lb.	=	?
Total equivalent weight of grass			=	

Two populations may be the same size and may even have the same biological mass, but there may be great differences in the rate at which they consume resources in their environment. Obviously, the population which makes the largest demands on its environment will use the most materials and produce the most waste. It is estimated by some conservationists that a North American in the United States uses fifty times more resources than a native of India. In terms of polluting his environment, the North American has a far more devastating effect. Not only does he use more from his own environment, he also uses materials imported from distant places. His technology produces wastes which are not easily broken down and returned to nature. Such wastes as plastic containers, aluminum cans, and toxic chemical products pollute America far more than the wastes of an Indian pollute India.

The pressures put upon land by advanced societies is also important. Most advanced societies obtain proteins from animals rather than from plants. A North American who has bacon and eggs for breakfast is consuming animal protein which was produced only after the hogs and chickens fed upon grain from green plants. But an Asian who eats rice is directly consuming green plants products. The transfer of energy from plants to domestic animals to man results in large energy losses. The pig or chicken uses food to reach its adult size and once it becomes fully grown continues to consume plant products. In the case of the hog, one unit of feed does not produce one unit of hog growth after the animal matures. Only a nation with ample land resources can afford the luxury of having herds or flocks of mature animals to supply it with animal protein. Only the people of two countries— United States and Canada—depend on animal protein for more than one-half of their total protein intake. As the ratio of land to people shrinks due to increased numbers of persons, it is necessary for people to rely more and more upon plants for their proteins.

A FISH STORY

Recapture Counting

How many marbles are there in a bucketful of marbles? One way to find out is to count every marble. If there are thousands of marbles, the job will be time-consuming. But if you don't need an exact number for your answer, the job can be made easier by estimating the number. There are several ways you can learn to estimate the number of individuals in a population. One way is called the recapture method because you keep recapturing individuals that you have marked. Try this.

Place 190 marbles of one color in a pail. Add ten equal-size marbles of a different color. We will call the ten marbles of a different color the marked marbles. Mix the marbles thoroughly. Now, without looking, reach into the bucket and take out ten marbles. Count the number of marked marbles and record that number in a chart like the one shown. Replace the ten and mix the marbles. Repeat this process ten times. Calculate the percentage of marked marbles in each sample and find the average percentage of marked marbles. By using some arithmetic, you can calculate the number of marbles in the bucket. Then you can compare the calculated number with the actual number of marbles in the bucket. Are the results of the estimate different if you use 170 marbles of one color and 30 of another?

Recapture

Trial	# of Marked Marbles	# in Sample	% of Marked Marbles
1	?	10	?
2	?	10	?
3	?	10	?
4	?	10	?
5	?	10	?
6	?	10	?
7	?	10	?
8	?	10	?
9	?	10	?
10	?	10	?

Average % of marked marbles =

Let us put our experiment with the marbles to use. Suppose a biologist wants to learn how many fish there are in a small stretch of stream. But fish, being elusive animals, are not like the marbles in the bucket. The biologist has a net which can capture only a limited number of fish at one time. The biologist blocks both ends of the stream and begins to capture fish. He clips a tiny portion out of the dorsal fin of each captured fish. This mark is too small to affect the movements of the fish, but clear enough so that he can recognize the fish in the future. He returns the marked fish to the stream and continues to net and mark any unmarked fish. At some point, he notices that most dips of his net show close to 50 percent marked fish. Cleverly, he has kept a total count of all the marked fish.

Now he is ready to begin his population estimate. He nets about one hundred fish four or five times. Each time, he notes the number of marked to unmarked fish in his net. He obtains the following percent of marked fish each time: 43 percent, 45 percent, 46 percent, 44 percent, 47 percent. Again he makes a series of five dips and finds 34, 48, 42, 45, and 56. The average number of marked fish turns out to be 45 percent. If he marked 450 fish, then the unmarked fish in the stream must be about 550 fish. The total fish population would be close to one thousand. One month later he comes back and finds a lower percent of marked fish in his five samples 35, 45, 32, 40, and 48. Does this mean that the population is lower? Or that some new fish have taken the place of marked and unmarked fish? What happens to his estimate if a fish-eating bird takes up residence in the area? What happens if a flood hits the stream? What happens if a boy nets minnows and sells them for bait? Will pollution in the stream change the population or the percent of the marked fish in his sample?

A PICTURE IS WORTH A THOUSAND

Photo Censusing

What is the population of this stadium? Using a magnifying glass and some graph paper you can make a close estimate of the number of people in the photograph.

Understanding a population usually depends upon knowing how many individuals it contains. This is true for both plants and animals. Plants usually occur in huge numbers, and counting them is a problem because there are so many. Animals, on the other hand, are difficult to count because they move about, causing people who count them to miss some and count some twice. Some kinds of animals, such as big-game animals, may be photographed when they concentrate in herds, provided they do not hide themselves under trees. These photographs are studied and counts are made from the photograph. The members of the herd must be close enough together so that a single picture, or a series taken from the air, includes all the members.

This technique works especially well for mammals and birds that live on treeless sea islands. A plane or helicopter flies over the population at a height which does not frighten or scatter the animals. The problem of double counts and misses which might occur if a herd was in motion and was being counted by a ground observer is eliminated. Often caribou are counted by photo censusing as they travel over the treeless tundra, and zebras are photographed as they gallop across the African plains. This method cannot be used in woodlands or for small mammals and birds because they are concealed by the plants and because they are so small that they do not show up in photographs.

There are many advantages to photo censusing. The airplane or helicopter allows the census-taker to follow the population over ground where land vehicles could not travel safely or swiftly. Also, pictures made at ground level often miss counting animals hidden from view by other animals, but the aerial view of the herd avoids this problem.

The photo-censusing technique is not limited to animals. Large plants, such as trees, can also be censused from the air. Pictures of trees made when flying over woodlands are helpful in identifying kinds of trees. This is done by studying differences in color or tone. Measurements of the tree shadows on the photo help the viewer find the height of the trees, but do not reveal the trees' age. Evergreen trees show up readily in woodlands photographs when the deciduous trees have shed their leaves. Certain kinds of deciduous trees, such as beech and sycamore, have very light bark which allows them to be distinguished from other deciduous trees. If pictures are made in color during the fall, more species can be recognized than when the trees are leafless.

TWO'S COMPANY

Overcrowding

What happens to the growth of plants that are un-crowded? Slightly crowded? Very crowded? Using equal-size pots and equal amounts of the same soil in each pot, plant lima-bean seeds in this way: one bean each in four pots, four beans in one pot, sixteen beans in one pot, and thirty-two beans in one pot. Let them grow until two of the plants in the 32-bean pot begin to show yellowing or breakage.

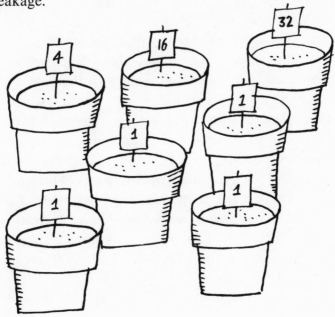

Find the weight of the plants in each pot and the average weight of each plant in pots 4, 16, and 32. Do the plants that grew singly weigh more than each one that grew in the other pots?

Populations are affected by many factors such as disease, severe weather conditions, and predation. It is possible to classify these factors into two basic groups. First, there are factors that take a fixed percentage toll of the population. A tropical storm, for instance, might destroy 10 percent of the birds nesting on a series of islands. It would not matter whether the island had one hundred pairs of nesting birds or one thousand pairs of nesting birds—on each island about 10 percent of the birds would be destroyed. The severe weather does not destroy the birds on the larger island any more or less than it destroys the birds on a smaller island. We classify the severe weather factor as "density-independent," because it causes a fixed proportion of destruction.

The second basic group is that where the size of the population has something to do with the ill effect. It is called "density-dependent." For instance, a disease may destroy more animals in a large, crowded population than in a small, scattered population. As a population becomes crowded, animals come into closer touch with each other and have more opportunities to transmit a disease. And stresses from crowding often make a population more susceptible to disease. Under crowded conditions, mother rats are more careless about caring for their young which may be killed by other rats if not properly defended.

There's an old saying, "Two's company, three's a crowd." Although it is not always easy to describe an overpopulated area, crowded populations show physical symptoms of distress. The members may fight more with each other, and examination of the adrenal glands often shows great enlargement when populations have been overcrowded. Crowding does not end until some members leave the population or die in the process of trying to survive.

WHAT'S MINE IS MINE

Territoriality

Who lives at the house out in the suburbs? Is it just the people in the house who are the inhabitants, or do the birds and squirrels have some claim to home ownership? And do the people allow just anyone to come in from the street and eat dinner or sleep in a bed? Do the birds and squirrels allow this also? Find out how birds feel about whose yard they live in by studying their actions toward new birds, or seemingly new birds, who might visit. Place a large mirror on the ground near a tree where you have often seen a robin. What does the robin do to the image of himself that he sees in the mirror?

What do dogs do when strange dogs enter their yards? Find a neighborhood dog who barks when he sees other dogs approaching. When does the "at home" dog stop barking and start fighting with the other dog? Crowding among animals is an unnatural condition. Many kinds of animals seem to live inside an invisible fence. If another of their own kind trespasses over the lines into their territory, they immediately react and try to drive away the invader.

The establishment of territory is one way in which populations of animals are regulated. Territories tend to reduce any overpopulation brought about by crowding.

We have seen that severe weather, a density-independent device, and crowding, a density-dependent device, both affect population control. Now let's see how territoriality acts as a population control.

Territoriality is based on the behavior of individuals. It can be defined as the defense of an area, within a large environment, that is used by one animal. Many animals live their whole life in a comparatively restricted area but actually defend a smaller portion of that area. This defense guarantees a minimum area needed to supply food for the growing family of the defender. It helps conserve energy for animals who are often under great stress to feed their growing young. Instead of animals fighting with each other over property boundaries, they usually recognize each other's boundaries. An established

pair of animals will usually fight with neighbors rather than with constantly roaming members of their population. And, they usually reach an agreement with their neighbors. In this way territorialism helps control population distribution. It may last only during the breeding season or it may be constant throughout the year. Unlike grouping together, which can have various survival values, territoriality reduces competition by enabling pairs of animals to have their own "homes."

Many theories have been suggested to explain territoriality. Since territorialism varies from the defense of just the immediate nesting site, as in seabirds, to the defense of areas much larger than that needed to supply food, theories about its conserving food may explain only some kinds of territoriality.

THE DIFFICULT YEARS

Infant Mortality

Do more children survive now than did one or two hundred years ago? What percentage of all those who died during the past fifty years were younger than five years old? During the fifty years before that? And fifty years before that? One way to study this question is to study the dates on tombstones in a cemetery. By using a chart and a little mathematics, you can decide whether more young children survive now than did in the past.

Period	Number of Tombstones	% of
Most-recent-fifty-year period 1950–2000	# of tombstones whose persons were 5 or younger	% of 5 years or younger
	# over 5 years old	% of over 5-year-olds
Second-most-recent-fifty-year period 1900–1950	# of tombstones whose persons were 5 or younger	%
	# over 5 years old	%
Third-most-recent-fifty-year period 1850–1900	# of tombstones whose persons were 5 or younger	%
	# over 5 years old	%

When animals are young they are very vulnerable. Lacking size, experience, and adult defenses, a young animal cannot successfully compete with adults, and in many species can survive only with much care from its parents. The young plant seedling is also at a sensitive stage of development. With its soft tissues, there is poor mechanical protection for the young plant against wind or trampling.

The mortality of young animals or tender young plants is usually greater than at any other stage of life of the organism. Since all organisms must grow through this critical stage if they are to reach maturity, it is a stage of life that has many problems. Events that affect young organisms play a crucial role in population success. And, if every young animal or every seedling survived, the world's space would soon be filled with organisms beyond any capacity to support them. Perhaps in the scheme of nature it is less wasteful of energy if the small immature organisms perish rather than if older ones die because little time or energy has been invested in their growth.

Throughout the world where human beings are starving, it is invariably the infants and small children who are the first to die. They are the ones that suffer when their parents are unable to give them the minimum food, medicine, and healthy surroundings needed for proper development. The great surging growth of the human race has been brought about mainly by saving human infants rather than by extending the time that adults live. A high human birth rate made sense when few children lived to reach adulthood. Such a birth rate was built into the evolution of man as a protection against extinction. Today, the excess children that once died now survive and find increasingly smaller amounts of food and space to share. Although this cruel fact is everywhere, it is most obvious in the underdeveloped countries—the countries which do not have enough resources to support their populations.

BILL OF FARE

Food Resources

Do people feel better when they eat as much as they like of one kind of food or when they only eat a limited amount of several different kinds of food? Does eating only one specific kind of food have detrimental effects on health? Since it doesn't make sense to try experimenting with human beings in order to answer these questions, it may be best to ask knowledgeable people about these ideas. Here are a series of questions that may be helpful for interviews aimed at understanding these ideas. When asking the questions, be sure to think about *who* is answering and group the answers according to some categories.

Questions:

- What harm can come from a diet that consists only of cereals?
- What are the advantages of a diet that includes a large amount of protein (meat, fish, eggs)? The disadvantages?
- Do people act differently when they eat whatever they want than when they eat some specific diet?

- Do people have food preferences that are "best" for their own nutritional well being?
- Are some foods harmful to one person and beneficial to others?

Some categories of answerers:

Mothers, fathers, teen-agers, grandmothers, young children, chefs, or cooks, grocerymen, doctors, college students.

The most interesting parts of the world are the places where variety thrives—variety of landscape, variety of life, and variety of ideas. Variety allows us to make choices. We like to feel that we can choose. In the crowded parts of our planet, choice is limited. The struggle to fill the stomach with one good meal a day is always present. The choice of a meal may be rice—or rice—or rice. The choice is not between pork chops or steak. It may be a choice between grasshoppers or grubs, and sometimes the choice must be uncooked instead of cooked because there is no fuel for cooking.

Throughout the world the plants known as grasses yield the grains of wheat, rice, corn, millet, and oats. Without these plants there would be no easy source of food for animals. If everyone would agree to live on large quantities of cereal, a fantastically large number of people might be fed. But was man designed to live on cereals? Can he digest them without first grinding them, or soaking the grains and boiling or baking them? Can he easily digest raw meat? All of these questions concern the problem of how many people the earth can support.

63

The illustration below shows that more organisms can be supported when food chains are short, that is,

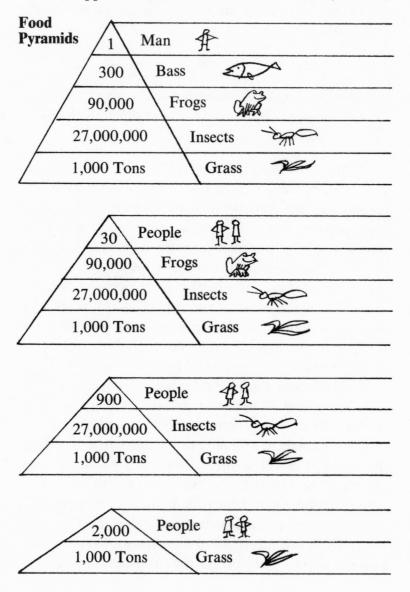

Food Pyramids

1	Man	
300	Bass	
90,000	Frogs	
27,000,000	Insects	
1,000 Tons	Grass	

30	People	
90,000	Frogs	
27,000,000	Insects	
1,000 Tons	Grass	

900	People	
27,000,000	Insects	
1,000 Tons	Grass	

2,000	People	
1,000 Tons	Grass	

when energy is passed from plants to a single group of ultimate animal consumers. As energy is passed up the food chain in the food pyramid, most of it is lost at each step upward in the process of growth and maintenance of each organism. The actual weight of organisms produced is always a small percentage of the plants or animals that are consumed as food. For the earth to achieve the maximum carrying capacity of people, they would have to obtain all their proteins from plants.

What would the world be like if man decided to manage the food resources of the earth so that the largest number of people could survive? First of all, any other users of green plants—deer, zebras, or mice—would have to be eliminated. If this were actually to happen, there would be no more zoos in the world because there would be no wild stocks of animals for stocking them.

The tigers, lions, wolves, foxes, and bears would find no prey because man would have eliminated all the other animals on which they feed. The landscape would be clothed with waving fields of grain—no wild flowers, few if any trees, and certainly few if any ornamental plants such as rose bushes or daffodils. Forget hamburgers, hot dogs, and roast turkeys because a maximum human population cannot be fed on meat. Both the diet and the landscape would be incredibly different than they are now, and they would probably be quite monotonous.

HOW OLD IS A MOMMY?

Population Growth Patterns

Finding out about population growth patterns can begin with something as easy as talking to the parents of families in your community. Armed with some system of classifying information, you can find out the general population patterns that exist among the people who live near you. Here are some questions and a sample of one system for gathering information:

1. How old was each parent of a family when the oldest child was born? The youngest?
2. Would the family feel crowded if another child was born?
3. How many children are there in the family?
4. Does the family expect to have more children?
5. Design a question of your own.

```
┌─────────────────────────────────────────────────────┐
│                  Information card                     │
│                                                       │
│   Family #1                                           │
│                                                       │
│   1. Age of mother. _____  _____        │
│                     youngest child   oldest child     │
│      Age of father. _____  _____        │
│                     youngest child   oldest child     │
│   2. Would another child crowd the home?              │
│      Yes____No____                                    │
│   3. Number of children in the family._____    │
│   4. More children expected?  Yes____No____           │
│      How many?_____                            │
│                                                       │
└─────────────────────────────────────────────────────┘
```

From this information you can find out:

1. The average childbearing age of the people you interviewed.
2. Their feelings about how large their family should be.
3. Their feeling about what is a "crowded" condition.

To produce a child takes a mother and father. In all higher animals, there must be a father and a mother to produce offspring. The more individuals of childbearing age in a population, the greater the possibilities for large numbers of offspring. In the human race, very old women and very young girls cannot have babies even if they are married to men who can father children. Young boys and very old men cannot father children even if they are married to women who could bear them.

In some cultures child marriages are arranged by parents. The young boys and girls go through a marriage ceremony, but do not have children until they grow up. In other words, only physically mature people can have children. A woman, for instance, may begin to bear children in her early teens and continue to do so until her forties or early fifties. For a woman who lives to the age of eighty years, only three decades out of the eight are ones in which she may bear children. For a man, who lives until age eighty, it is possible to father children from teen-age onward. For most of his life, he is able to father children.

If a population is made up of a high percentage of reproductive individuals, those in the childbearing age, it tends to grow faster than one in which a low percentage is found. Cultural patterns which delay marriages reduce human reproduction. This is the case in Ireland where men marry at age thirty-five or older and women at about age twenty-five. By contrast, people in Mexico marry at an early age and the population growth rate there is quite different than it is in Ireland. Population growth in countries such as Mexico soon cancels out gains made in housing, food supply, and other areas.

Most families in North America try to limit the number of children to those for which they can provide care. The ability to provide care varies with each family. It is unfortunate when a family produces more children than can receive the care which they need. Producing children is something that any healthy mature man and woman can do, but providing care calls for skills, space, and resources which vary among individuals, families, and countries.

EAT UNTIL WE BURST

Population Explosions

How dependent is man's population growth on his ability to gather and use food? Here are some tasks to try which might help you understand our dependency on food technology:

- Don't eat any meat for three days *unless* you catch it yourself. (Rabbits, fish, etc.)
- What foods, usable in their natural state, are available in your geographic area during each season? Devise a diet based only on these foods.
- Find out how many foods that you eat come from areas not more than fifty miles from your home.
- What percentage of all the food you eat comes from areas more than fifty miles from your home?
- List all of the nonfarming jobs there are that must be done in order for you to buy roast beef in a supermarket.
- Look at all the foods purchased for your family and decide which of them are necessities and which are luxuries that give little food value.

When man first developed from his primitive ancestors, he progressed rapidly because he learned to use and
make tools. Chimpanzees have been observed to use
twigs to get ants from their burrows. This primate rela-
tive of man probably uses no other kinds of tools. But the

caveman who learned to make and hurl spears and fashion bows and arrows became a successful hunter. These techniques enabled early man to gather wild meat. Although he could capture this meat, he had little or no influence on how much was available because he had no way of increasing the supply.

In the great surge of the world's human population, man deliberately set out to control his food supply by planting and caring for it. His early ancestors may have depleted the vast herds of plant eaters which fed him when he was a hunter. Or perhaps he realized that grains could be stored, but meat would rot. Using fire, he extracted the energy in the grains which gave him his daily bread or was used to feed domestic animals. Agriculture gave man the time to develop his culture.

Another surge of human population developed when man reached back into the past for energy stored there by biological processes. Coal and oil fueled his industrial revolution. The energy that man used was released from organic molecules, ones created by past life.

Today man once again may be prepared to experience a great surge in population because he now extracts energy from inorganic nuclear fuels. Only time will tell whether such energy can be safely released to benefit man.

FOUR NOTES OF SUMMARY

Where
Will
It Go?

From what you have learned in this book, it is possible to put together many ideas and see how they apply to man. The human population is a special case of population. Let's look at some of the major concerns of people who are interested in the human population crisis.

The biological rules that apply to the growth of human populations are the same that apply to other kinds of population. The main difference between the human population and other populations, such as deer or lettuce, is that the human population has never stopped growing for long. Once in the 1300s, when the "black death" (bubonic plague) struck Europe, a temporary dip in human numbers took place. We humans have continued to grow in numbers ever since. In the process we have destroyed populations of many other kinds of animals which once shared the earth with us.

Is there a perfect number of people to make a world population? No one has really defined what an optimum population should be. Suppose that we arbitrarily assume that the best population for the world is one which would enable all people to enjoy the living standards that now prevail in the United States. If we choose such a standard for all, then it is estimated that the entire world could support a population of only one billion people. This is less than 30 percent of the three and one-half billion people who presently exist on the earth.

If this is true, and one billion is the optimum world population, then raising hopes for an "American standard of living" is a cruel dream to dangle in front of the world's starving and ill-fed. By seeing films and television, the underprivileged people of the world now understand for the first time in the history of the world how comfortable and safe life can be. The language barrier no longer prevents them from understanding what goes on, because their eyes tell them all they need to know. Will this lead to a "population revolution" based on peoples' rising hopes? No one can be sure. Is the desire for a better life important enough to people that they will regulate their populations and not destroy the environment which provides for their needs? It would appear that those who lack modern standards of living will never achieve them if they continue to follow historic patterns of human growth. Also, those who presently enjoy high standards of living may be entering an age when such standards will decline. This decline will occur when world resources will have to be divided among more and more people.

Concern with population problems has led to the formation of such organizations as Zero Population Growth, Inc. (ZPG). The goal of this organization is to have people adjust births so they do not exceed deaths. This would prevent man from overwhelming the earth with his ever-expanding human population. It is too early to say how successful groups of this kind will be in convincing their fellow humans to adopt such a goal. But the projections made by demographers (people who measure population) indicate that the world population is growing at a sharply accelerating pace which shows no sign of halting.

The
Rare and
Threatened
Species

Many species of animals are threatened by man today. It is not only because man still hunts them for food, but also because he has destroyed so much of their environment that they no longer have a secure place in which to live.

Neither large numbers, nor great physical strength, nor size can enable a species to survive the onslaught of man. Passenger pigeons existed in unbelievably large flocks not many years ago. Not a single one remains today. It is estimated that forty-five million bison occupied North America in 1600, with some herds numbering as large as two million animals. Today only a token population of bison exists on fenced-in preserves. Species of great strength or stealth, such as the grizzly bear and mountain lion, have been drastically reduced or exterminated over most of their former range. Our national emblem, the bald eagle, has become a rare breeding bird within the forty-eight adjoining states although numbers still survive in Alaska. In the case of the eagle, DDT has so seriously interfered with normal egg production that eggs cannot succeed in hatching.

Whooping cranes number less than one hundred birds in all of the United States, and they are barely surviving. Their wintering grounds at Aransas, Texas, are threatened by man's expanded activities near their sanctuary. Alligators in the United States and crocodiles throughout the world are threatened by poachers who seek their hides and by land development that changes their homes. The same problem plagues the large spotted cats of the world—the leopard, jaguar, tiger, snow leopard, and others. The destruction of such animals satisfies the vanity of man and provides furs of poor durability, however fashionable they may be at times.

Ultimately man could eliminate almost every large creature on earth. The largest ones are the easiest to find and capture or destroy. The tiny associates of man and his domestic animals, such as the rat, the cockroach, and the housefly, will never be endangered species in spite of attempts to eliminate them with all the modern methods of man's technology. Without concern for the rare and vanishing species of this world, coupled with the conscious protection of their environments, man's growing population will destroy the many varied forms of life which share the planet with him.

Man as a Threatened Species

During a recent observance of Earth Day, a zoo exhibited a cage containing man amid piles of trash and garbage. The zoo's idea was that man is already a threatened species. Not only is man a threatening species to other forms of life, but his very numbers and the decline in the quality of his life due to excess crowding threatens his own existence.

Man has become so great a modifier of the earth's surface that he now rivals natural geologic agents in changing the face of the earth. His influence stretches from the depths of the oceans where he deposits atomic wastes to the atmosphere where condensation trails from jets could lead to changes in the earth's climate by the filtering effect on sunlight.

The toxic substances of the earth, such as arsenic, lead, and mercury, which were once firmly locked into the solid crust of the earth, can now circulate uncontrolled all over the globe. The accumulation of these toxic substances in the flesh of organisms appears to be growing. Synthetic substances such as DDT and dieldrin, both man-made organic chemicals originally created to control insects, now persist and travel uncontrollably throughout the world.

Large amounts of cancer-producing hydrocarbons steadily enter the ocean each day from work and pleasure ships. The petroleum products are taken up by many forms of ocean life which man uses for food. It has become virtually impossible to find a stretch of ocean which is not contaminated to some extent with petroleum products.

Before man continues to pollute the world with substances of potentially great harm, he needs to find out more about them. Then he can use these substances in ways that will prevent disasters. Human wastes, for example, have created problems from the time that smoke from fires polluted the first cave. But, the nature and extent of toxic substances released by man today exceeds all of the methods we have for absorbing and cleaning the land, sea, and air.

One last view of man as a threatened species might be thought about. Man could turn out to have the questionable distinction of being the shortest-lived species in the fossil record of the world. But the brain which would cause this extinction would also keep him from disappearing—if he wanted it to.

The
Final
Outcome

Man alone in the animal world has the ability to foresee the consequences of his acts. Usually he doesn't choose to see them. He can make the choice of developing a world fit for himself and all other passengers on the spaceship Earth or he may ignore that choice.

The condition of the world in which man lives depends upon three factors: 1) the size of his population; 2) the objects and services that each person requires for a meaningful, safe, and interesting life; and 3) the stresses imposed upon the land, water, and air in the course of making material objects and performing services to meet each person's need. All three of these factors interact together. All three factors can be controlled by human choices.

Any given area of the earth can support different mixtures of these three factors. If people are numerous, but demand little and do not use technology in an environmentally costly way, they will not destroy their environment. A moderately sized population with large demands for goods and services can quickly destroy its resources. Each person added to such a demanding and destructive culture quickens the ultimate destruction of that person. The deteriorating quality of man's environment will eventually perform the necessary task of stabilizing human populations. In the past, wars, famine, and disease did much the same kind of job. No one knows just how such factors will operate to limit the numbers of man, but one thing is certain: *there are upper limits for human populations as there are for every living thing.* Man *can* adjust his numbers in a humane and fair way which favors a life worth living, a life of choice, a life of interesting surroundings, and a life of unlimited creative and meaningful pursuits. Or, he may act without direction and inherit a dull, dirty, gray, lifeless world, where choice is absent, thinking stultified, and the growth of the human spirit finds a limit far beneath its capacity to dream and achieve.

SUGGESTED FURTHER READING

The following titles will be of interest to those concerned with the population explosion.

Drummond, A.H., Jr. *The Population Puzzle*. Reading: Addisonian Press, Addison-Wesley Publishing, 1973.

Fisher, Tadd. *Our Overcrowded World: A Background Book on the Population Explosion*. New York: Parents' Magazine Press, 1969.

Hyde, Margaret O. *This Crowded Planet*. New York: McGraw-Hill, 1961.

Rossman, Isadore. *Two Children By Choice*. New York: Parents' Magazine Press, 1970.

INDEX

Adrenal glands, 11, 55
Age profile, 20-23
Agriculture, 73
Alaska, 77
Alligators, 78
Aransas, Texas, 78

Balance of nature, 9, 10
Bald eagle, 77
Birds, 18, 19, 38-39, 42, 56, 77-78
Birth rate, 33, 60-61, 75
Bison, 25-26, 27, 77
Black rat, 29, 30
Brown rat, 30
Browse line, 11
Bubonic plague, 29, 74
Buck law, 18

Canada, 46
Cats, 18, 78

Census, 21
    photo censusing, 51-52
Cereals, 62, 63
Child mortality, 59-61
Childbearing, 67-70
Chimpanzees, 72
Compatibility of species, 28-30
Crocodiles, 78
Crowding, 1-2, 10-11, 53-55, 56, 79

DDT, 15, 77, 79-80
Deer, 10-11, 18, 42
Demographers, 76
Dieldrin, 79-80
Diet, 44, 45-46, 62-66, 71
Distribution patterns, 37-39
Dogs, 39, 44, 56

Eagle, 77
Earth Day, 79

Samples, statistical, 16, 40
Seabirds, 38
Seals, 18-19
Sex ratios, 16-18
Snow leopard, 78
Space, living, 7-8, 24-25
Starlings, 38-39
Synthetic substances, 79-80

Territoriality, 56-58
Tiger, 78
Tools, 72-73
Toxic substances, 79, 80
Trees, 52, 66

Underdeveloped countries,
    61, 75

United States, 45, 46, 77, 78
    standard of living, 75

Voles, 35-36

Wastes, human, 80
Weapons, 73
Whooping cranes, 78
Wolves, 38
Wood rat, 29
Workers, 22

Yellow-nosed vole, 35-36

Zero Population Growth,
    Inc. (ZPG), 75
Zoos, 65

ABOUT THE AUTHORS

A. Harris Stone received his B.S. degree from West Chester State College and his master's degree and doctorate in education from the University of Pennsylvania. He is now Professor of Science Education and Chairman of the Science Education Department at Southern Connecticut State College in New Haven.

Dr. Stone has written many popular books, among them *The Chemistry of a Lemon* and *The Last Free Bird*. He is the co-author of a science education textbook entitled *Teaching Children Science: An Inquiry Approach*.

Stephen Collins received his B.S. degree from Cornell University and his Ph. D. from Rutgers. He is now Professor of Biology at Southern Connecticut State College. An active naturalist and conservationist, Dr. Collins is an accomplished nature photographer and his work has appeared in many major reference books and magazines. He is the co-author of one previous book entitled *The Community of Living Things in Forest and Woodland*.

Dr. Collins lives in Bethany, Connecticut, with his wife and three children.